Monika Twelsiek

# Mein erstes Konzert
## My First Concert

57 leichte Vortragsstücke aus 5 Jahrhunderten
57 Easy Concert Pieces from 5 Centuries

CD-Einspielung: Vera Sacharowa

**ED 20969**
ISMN 979-0-001-17438-1

Mainz · London · Berlin · Madrid · New York · Paris · Prague · Tokyo · Toronto
© 2016 SCHOTT MUSIC GmbH & Co. KG, Mainz · Printed in Germany

# Inhalt / Contents

Impressum:
Bestellnummer: ED 20969
ISMN: 979-0-001-17438-1
ISBN: 978-3-7957-4515-8
Coverfoto: Vladislav Gajic
CD-Einspielung: Vera Sacharowa
Aufnahme: Studio Tonmeister, Mainz
© 2016 Schott Music GmbH & Co. KG, Mainz
BSS 54041 · Printed in Germany

# Vorwort

Das erste Konzert stellt für jede Instrumentalschülerin / für jeden Instrumentalschüler ein ganz besonderes Erlebnis dar. Die intensive Zeit der Vorbereitung, die Mischung aus Bangen und froher Erwartung, die Konzentration beim Auftritt, der Applaus des Publikums und der Stolz nach der gelungenen Leistung, all diese Eindrücke haften im Gedächtnis und sind nicht selten prägend für die gesamte weitere Entwicklung.

Dabei ist die Wahl des „richtigen" Vortragsstücks von entscheidender Bedeutung. Stücke für ein erstes Konzert sollten

- · nicht zu lang, aber auch nicht zu kurz sein,
- · eine gute Wirkung haben und Freude beim Üben machen,
- · technisch einfach, aber musikalisch anspruchsvoll und nicht langweilig sein.

Diesen Anspruch zu erfüllen stellt für Komponisten eine der schwierigsten Aufgaben dar. Ihre schönsten originalen Klavierstücke sind in diesem Heft gesammelt. Präsentiert werden kleine Werke großer Komponisten, darunter Bach und Händel, Haydn, Mozart und Beethoven, Chopin, Schumann, Grieg und Tschaikowsky, Bartók und Orff. Neben diesen berühmten Namen gibt es eine Fülle von Entdeckungen, kleine Meisterwerke, die den bekannteren Werken durchaus ebenbürtig sind.

Die Stücke sind nach Epochen und innerhalb der einzelnen Teile – Barock, Klassik, Romantik, Moderne, „Rock, Pop, Tango und mehr…" – nach Schwierigkeitsgraden geordnet. Die letzten Stücke jeden Kapitels stellen also jeweils kleine „Highlights" dar.

Ich wünsche allen Spielerinnen und Spielern Freude beim Üben und ein gelungenes erstes Konzert!

Monika Twelsiek

# Preface

Your first concert is a very special occasion for anyone learning to play an instrument. The time spent on intensive preparation, the mixture of fear and anticipation, heightened concentration on your performance, applause from the audience and then pride in your achievement – all these sensations will be remembered and may well mark the way for your future development.

Choosing the right piece is really important. Pieces for your first concert should be

- · neither too long, nor too short,
- · effective in performance and fun to work on,
- · technically undemanding, yet musically substantial and interesting.

Meeting this challenge represents one of the most difficult tasks for composers. Their finest original piano pieces are collected in this book. There are little pieces by great composers including Bach and Handel, Haydn, Mozart and Beethoven, Chopin, Schumann, Grieg and Tchaikovsky, Bartók and Orff. Besides these famous names there are other gems to discover, little masterpieces that are just as good as the better known works.

The pieces are grouped according to era of origin – Baroque, Classical, Romantic, Modern, Rock, Pop, Tango and more... – and presented in order of difficulty within each group. The last pieces in each chapter thus represent little concert highlights.

I wish all you pianists fun with your practice and a successful first concert!

Monika Twelsiek
Translation Julia Rushworth

# Barock / Baroque

## Alter deutscher Tanz / Old German Dance

Michael Praetorius
1571–1621

**1**

# Canario

Joachim von der Hofe
1567?–1620

**2**

# Gavotte

Georg Friedrich Händel
1685–1759

**3**

# Aria

Daniel Speer
1636–1707

**4**

# Menuett

Johann Krieger
1651–1735

**5**

*)

# Allemande

Johann Hermann Schein
1586–1630

**6**

# Bourrée

Christoph Graupner
1683–1760

**7**

# Gavotte en Rondeau

Jean-François Dandrieu
1682–1738

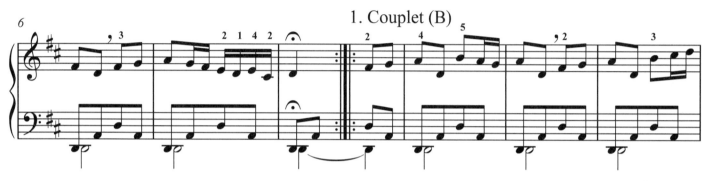

*) Spielfolge / Form: Refrain - Couplet 1 - Refrain - Couplet 2 - Refrain (A - B - A - C - A)

# Chaconne
## G-Dur / G major

Georg Friedrich Händel
1685–1759

**9**

# Präludium
## C-Dur / C major
### BWV 939

Johann Sebastian Bach
1685–1750

**10**

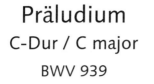

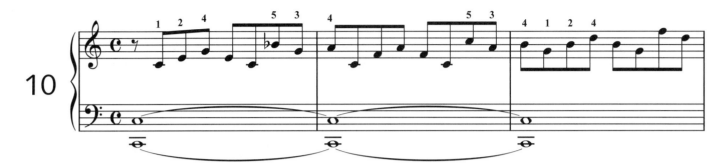

aus / from: J. S. Bach, 6 kleine Präludien aus der Sammlung Johann Peter Kellners /
6 little Preludes from the Peter Kellner Collection

# Klassik / Classical Age
# Vier kleine Stücke / Four Little Pieces

## I Entrée

Daniel Gottlob Türk
1756–1813

## II Minuetto

Daniel Gottlob Türk

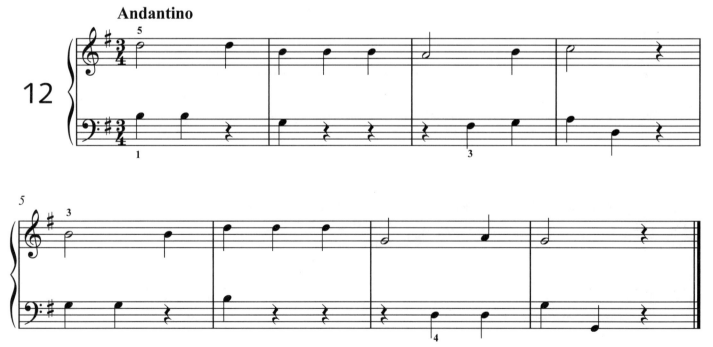

## III Ich bin so matt und krank / I am so Dull and Ill

Daniel Gottlob Türk

## IV Hanns ohne Sorgen / A Carefree Fellow

Daniel Gottlob Türk

# Drei kleine Stücke / Three Little Pieces

I

Antonio Diabelli
1781–1858

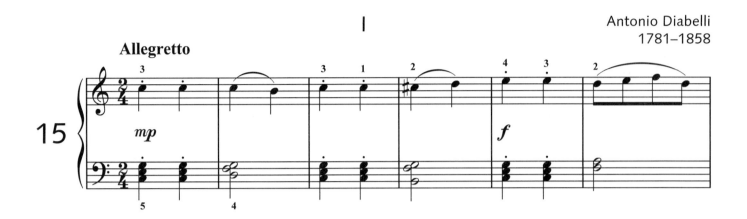

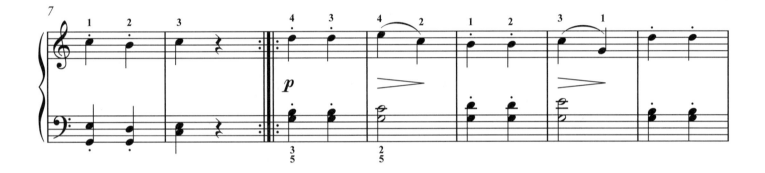

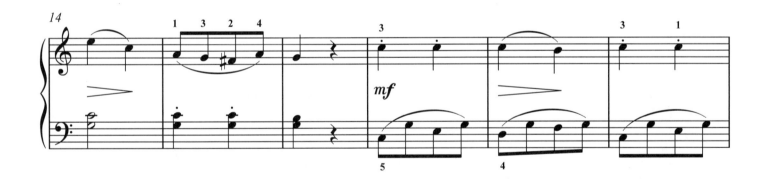

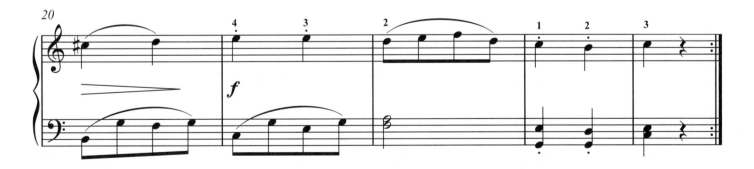

## II

Antonio Diabelli

**16**

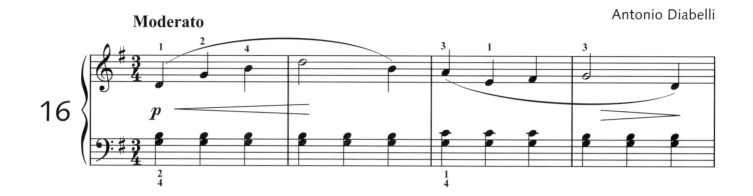

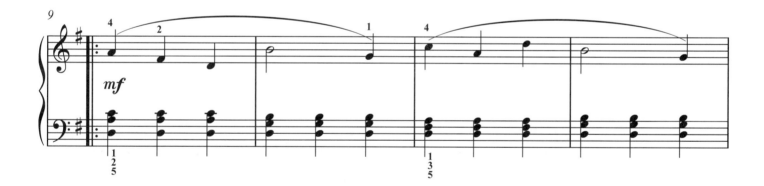

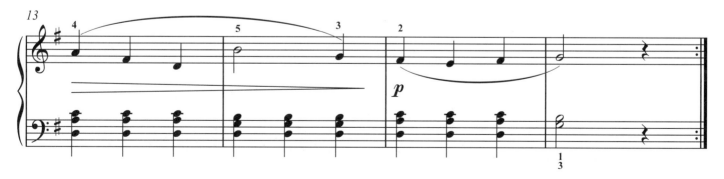

18

# III

Antonio Diabelli

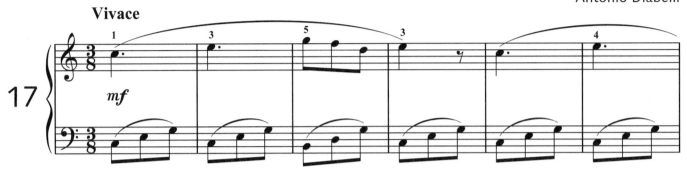

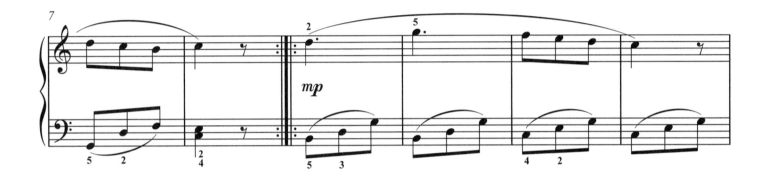

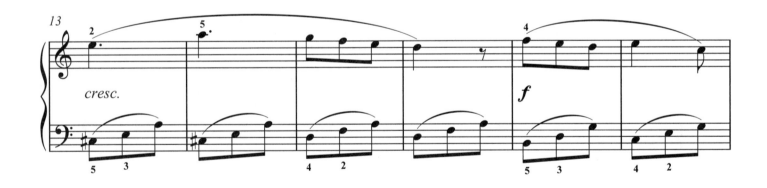

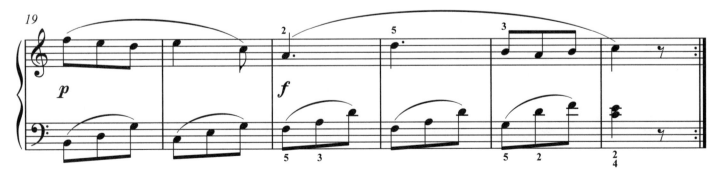

# Sonatine / Sonatina

## F - Dur / F major

### I

Johann Baptist Vanhal
1739–1813

**Andantino**

18

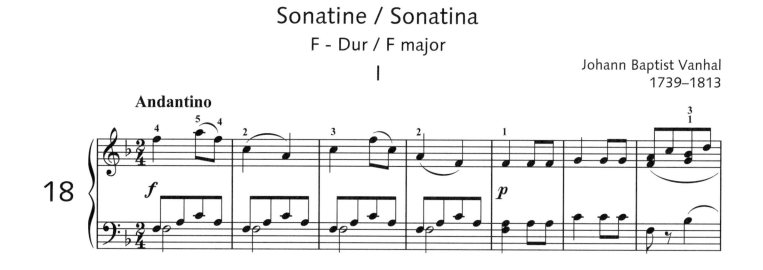

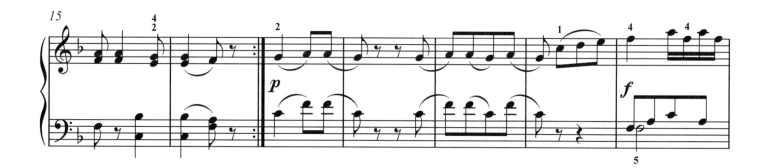

## II

**Allegretto**

**19**

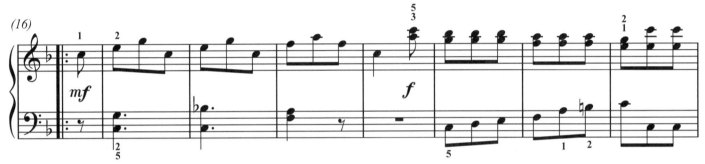

# Menuett

## F-Dur / F major

Joseph Haydn
1732–1809

**20**

aus / from: J. Haydn, 12 Menuette Hob IX:8, Nr. 11

# Die Schlittenfahrt / The Sleigh Ride

## KV 605/3

Wolfgang Amadeus Mozart
1756–1791

**21**

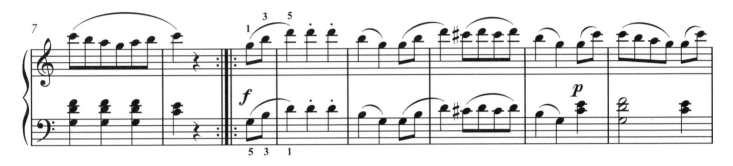

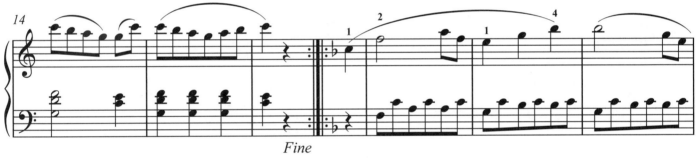

Fine

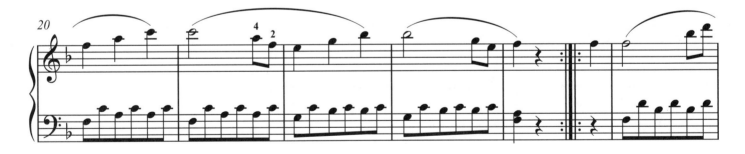

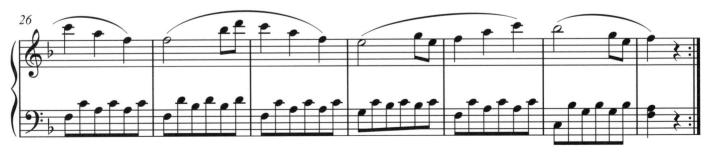

*D.C. al Fine*

aus / from: W. A. Mozart, Drei deutsche Tänze / Three German Dances KV 605

# Deutscher Tanz / German Dance
## C-Dur / C major

Ludwig van Beethoven
1770–1827

**22**

# Deutscher Tanz / German Dance
## G-Dur / G major

Ludwig van Beethoven

**23**

# Die Jagd / Hunting Jig

William Duncombe
1736–1818

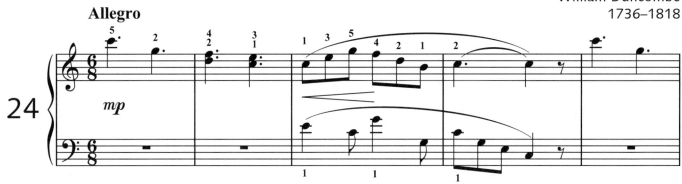

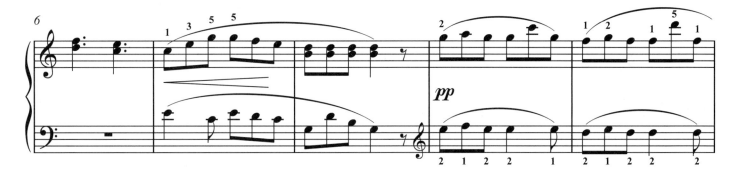

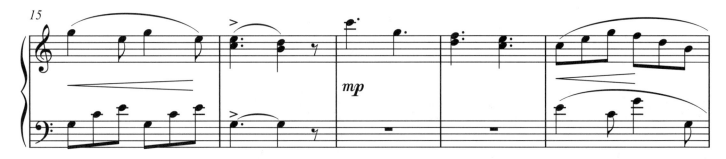

# Adagio
## a-Moll / A minor

Daniel Steibelt
1765–1823

**Gesanglich**

**25**

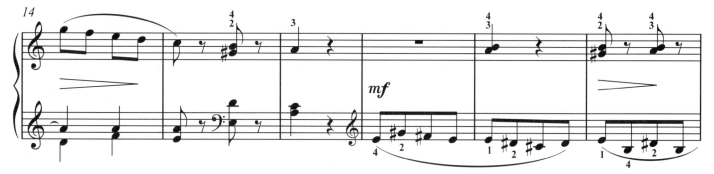

# Sonatine / Sonatina

## C-Dur / C major

### I

Tobias Haslinger
1787–1842

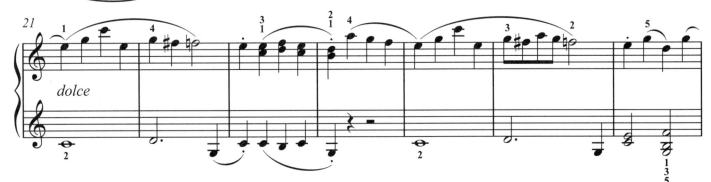

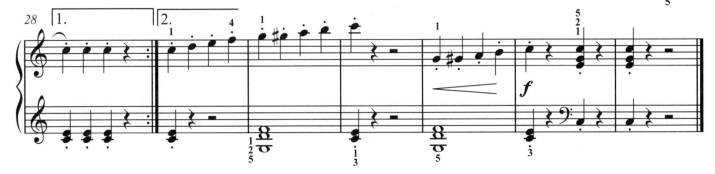

## II

Tobias Haslinger

**Allegretto**

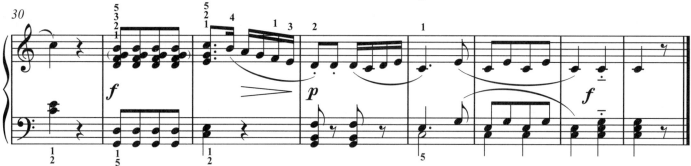

# Romantik / Romantic Age
## Lied ohne Worte / Song without Words

Fritz Spindler
1817–1905

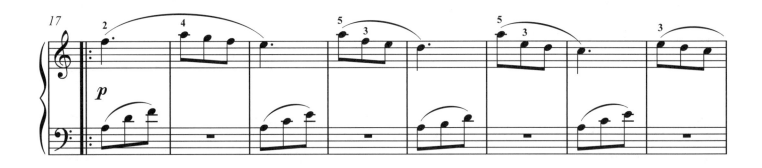

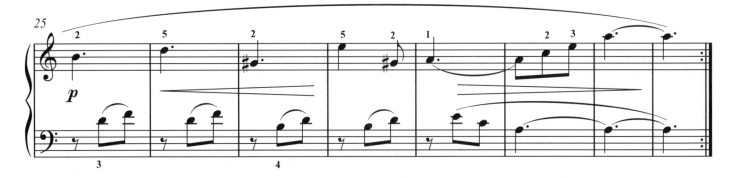

# Trübe Stunden / Dreary Hours

Cornelius Gurlitt
1850–1938

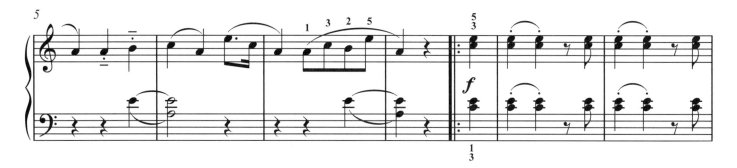

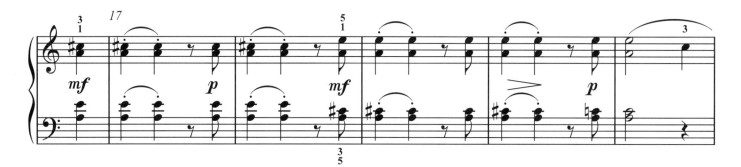

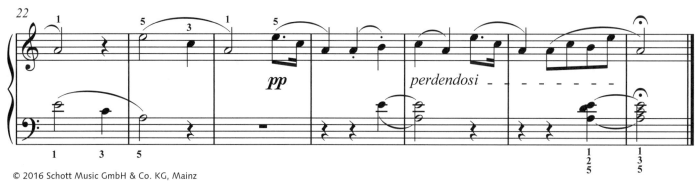

aus / from: C. Gurlitt, Der Hausfreund / The friend of the family op. 197

# Sommertagslied / A Midsommer Day's Song

Cornelius Gurlitt

**Allegretto**

aus / from: C. Gurlitt, Der Hausfreund / The friend of the family op. 197

# Ein kleines Märchen / Fairy Tale

Alexander Gretchaninoff
1864–1956

**31**

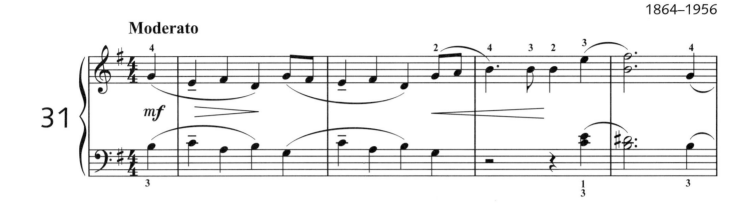

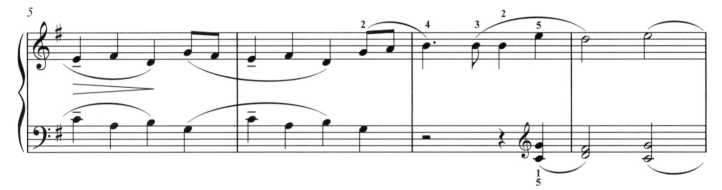

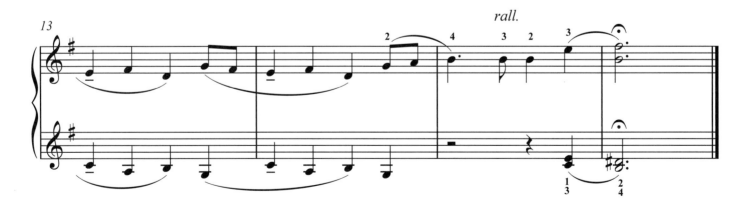

aus / from: A. Gretchaninoff, Das Kinderbuch / Children's Book op. 98, Schott ED 1100

# Eine langweilige Schularbeit / A Tiresome Lesson

Alexander Gretchaninoff

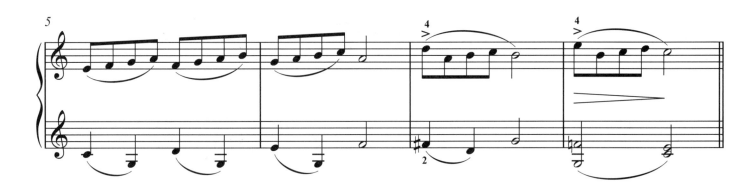

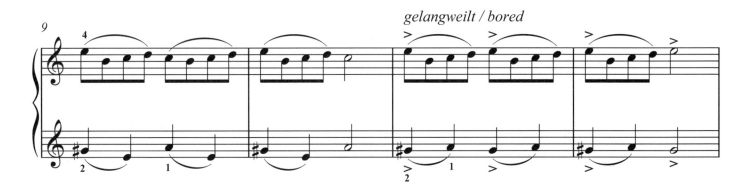

aus / from: A. Gretchaninoff, Das Kinderbuch / Children's Book op. 98, Schott ED 1100

# Altfranzösisches Lied / Old French Song

Peter Tschaikowsky
1840–1893

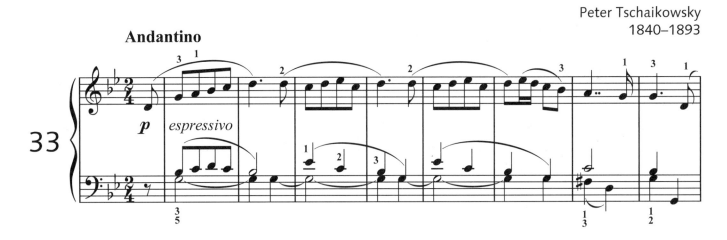

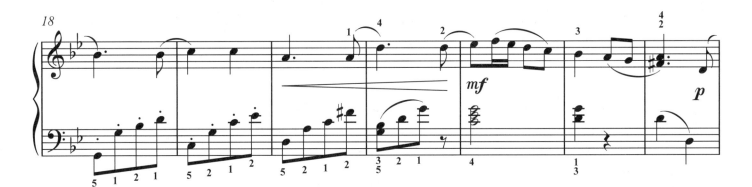

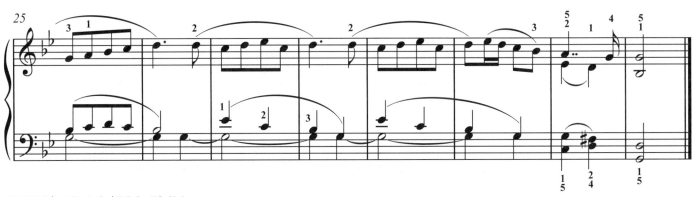

aus / from: P. Tschaikowsky, Kinderalbum / Children's Album, Wiener Urtext, UT 50134

# Der Puppe Klagelied / Dolly's Complaint

César Franck
1822–1890

**34**

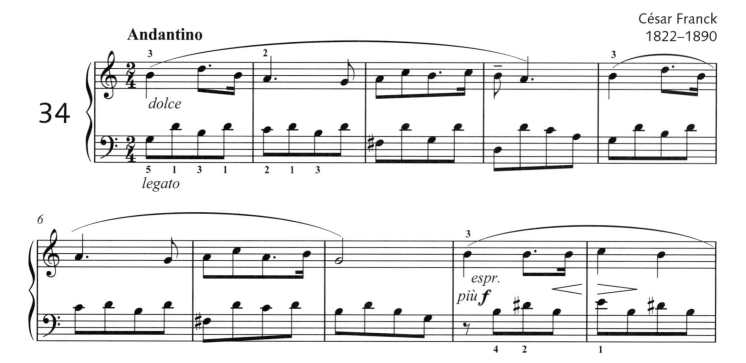
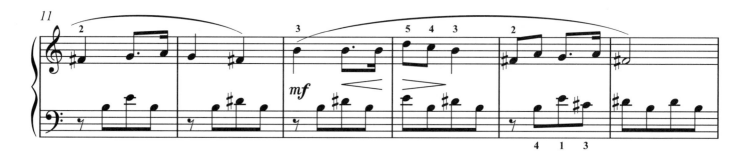

aus / from: C. Franck: 18 kurze Stücke / 18 Short Pieces / 18 petites pièces

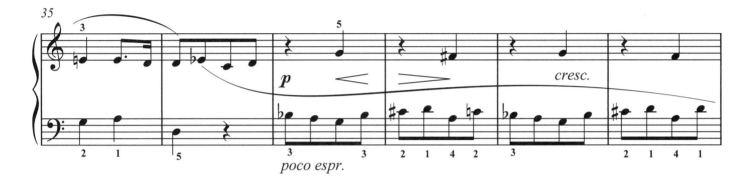

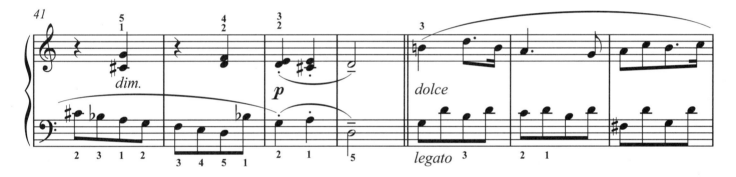

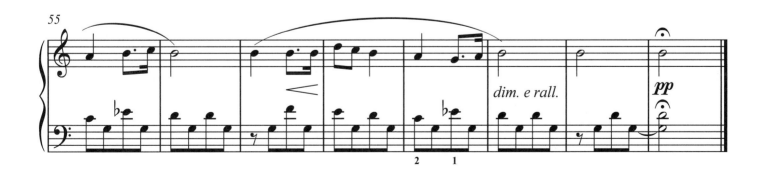

# Polnisches Lied / Polish Song

Frédéric Chopin
1810–1849

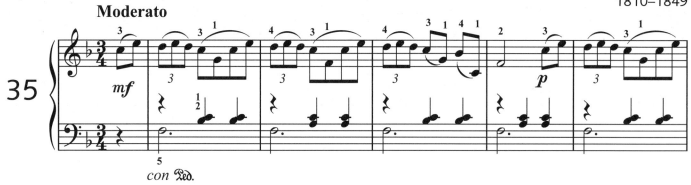

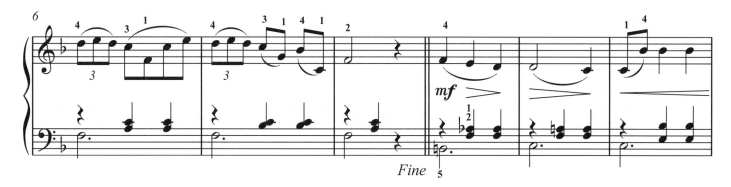

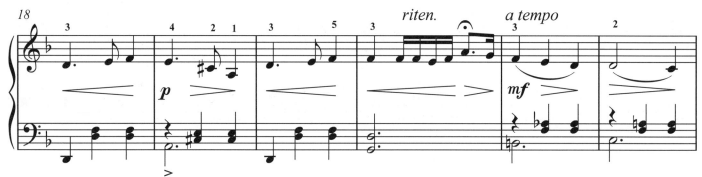

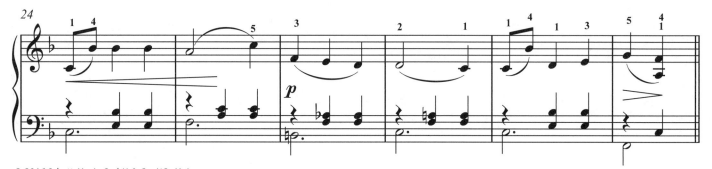

aus / from: F. Chopin, Polnische Lieder / Polish Songs op. 74/1

*D. C. al Fine*

# Stückchen / A Little Piece

Robert Schumann
1810–1856

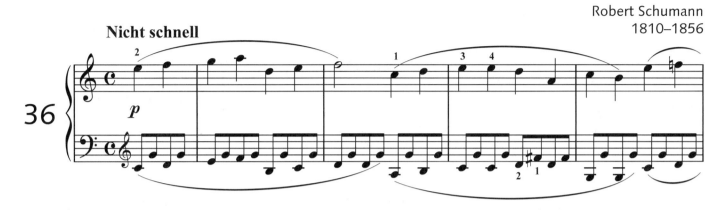

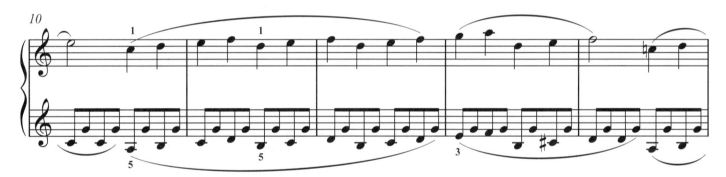

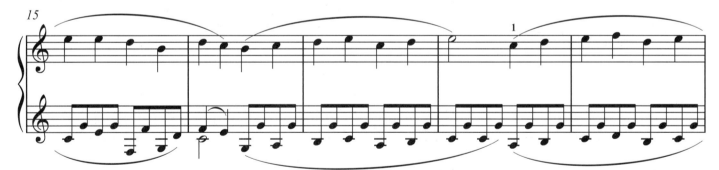

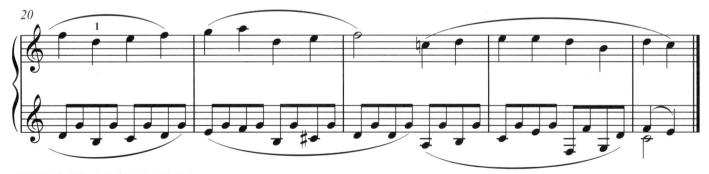

aus / from: R. Schumann, Album für die Jugend / Album for the Young, op. 68, Schott ED 9010

# Schnitterliedchen / Reaper's Song

Robert Schumann

**Nicht sehr schnell**

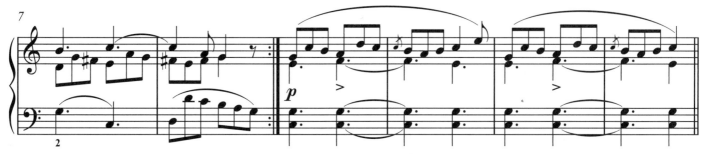

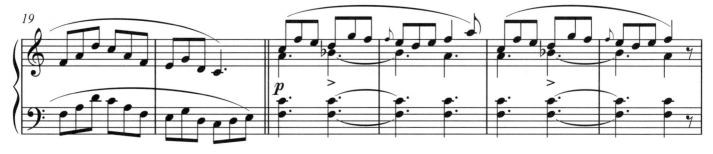

© 2016 Schott Music GmbH & Co. KG, Mainz
aus / from: R. Schumann, Album für die Jugend / Album for the Young, op. 68, Schott ED 9010

# Zarte Blume / The Tender Flower

Friedrich Burgmüller
1806–1874

**38**

aus / from: F. Burgmüller, 25 Etüden / 25 Studies op. 100, Schott ED 173

# Walzer / Waltz
## a-Moll / A minor

Edvard Grieg
1843–1907

**39**

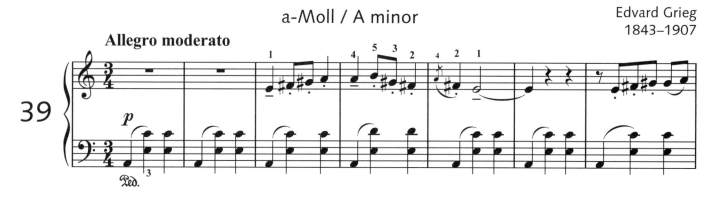

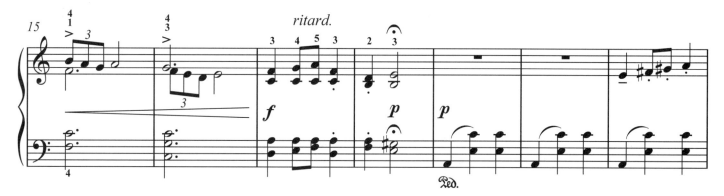

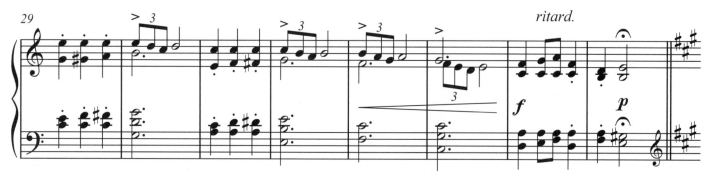

aus / from: E. Grieg, Lyrische Stücke / Lyric Pieces op. 112, ED 9012

# Moderne / Modern Age

## Die Eisenbahn / The Train

Georges Frank Humbert
1892–1958

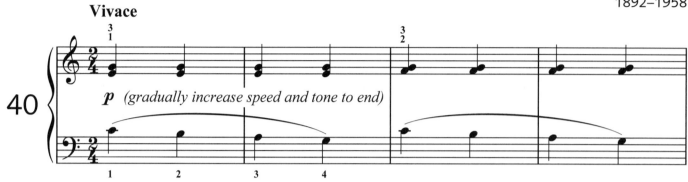

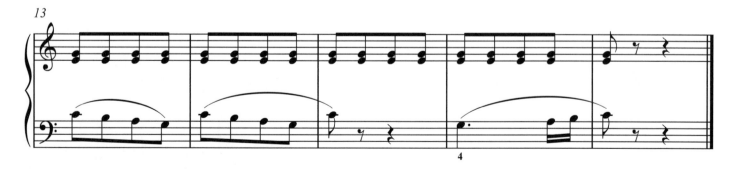

aus / from: G. F. Humbert, Allerlei Spielzeug / Toys, Schott ED 2605

## Elefanten / Elephants

Gunter Kretschmer
1935–2012

**Behäbig / Ponderously** ♩ = 80

41

aus / from: G. Kretschmer, Auf dem Spielplatz / In the Playground, Schott ED 20648

*) Hier kannst du die Elefanten ein Kunststück machen lassen.
   You can have the elephants do a trick here.

## Tanzstück / Dancing Piece

Carl Orff
1895–1982

42

*Fine*

*D. C. al Fine*

aus / from: C. Orff, Klavier-Übung, Schott ED 3561

44

## V Moderato

Béla Bartók
1881–1945

**Moderato** ($\quarternote$ = 66)

43

aus / from: B. Bartók, Erste Zeit am Klavier / First Term at the Piano

## VI Moderato

Béla Bartók

**Moderato** ($\quarternote$ = 108)

44

aus / from: B. Bartók, Erste Zeit am Klavier / First Term at the Piano

# Cantabile

Marko Tajčevič
1900–1984

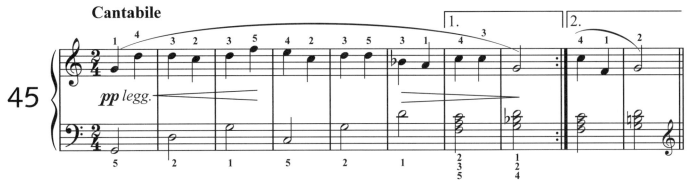

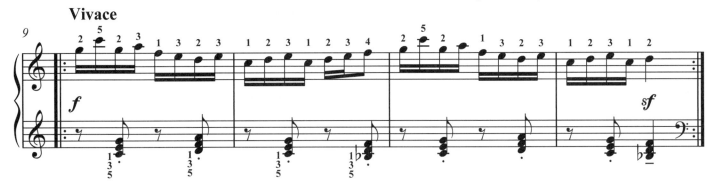

aus / from: M. Tajčevič, Für Kinder / For Children No. 4, Schott ED 21074

# In der Höhle / In the Cave

Hermann Regner
1928–2008

*) Der Abstand zwischen den Noten bedeutet relative Zeit. Wenn sie eng beieinander stehen, folgen sie schnell aufeinander; sind sie weiter voneinander entfernt notiert, kommen sie langsamer nacheinander.

*) The distance between the notes indicates the relative time. If the notes are close to each other they follow quickly one after the other; if they are further apart they follow each other more slowly.

aus / from: H. Regner, Es war einmal ein König / Once upon a time there was a King, Schott ED 8546

# Spiel / Play

Béla Bartók
1881–1945

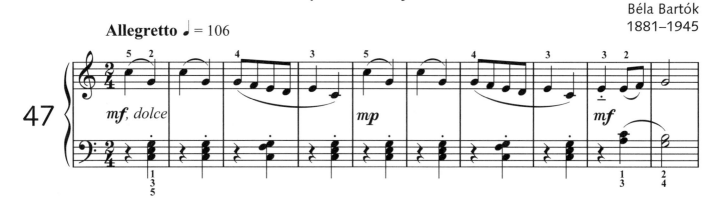

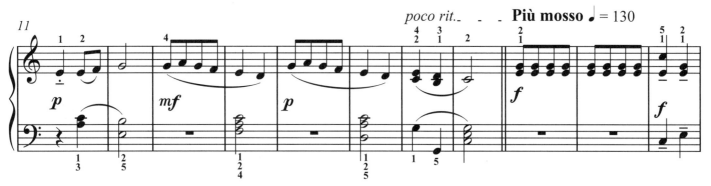

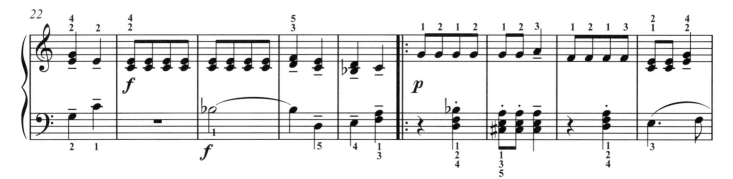

(1' 5")

aus / from: B. Bartók, Für Kinder / For Children

# Quasi adagio

Béla Bartók

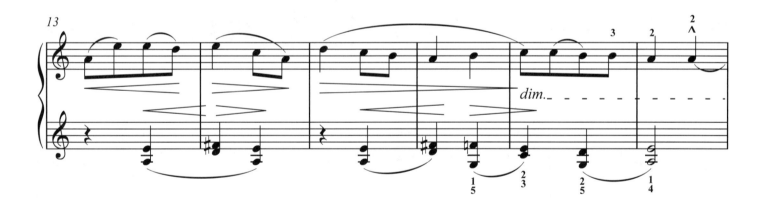

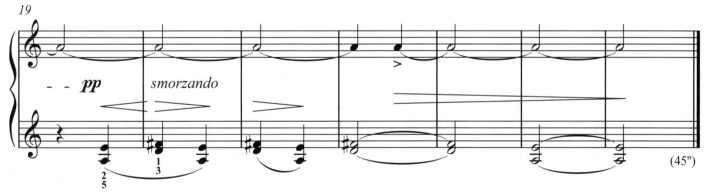

(45")

aus / from: B. Bartók, Für Kinder / For Children

# Kindertanz / Children's Dance

Béla Bartók

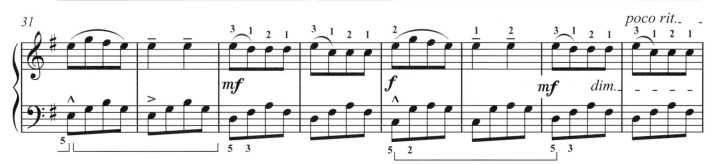

(40")

aus / from: B. Bartók, Für Kinder / For Children

# Der verzauberte Zwerg erwacht

## The Bewitched Dwarf Awakens

Rainer Mohrs
*1953

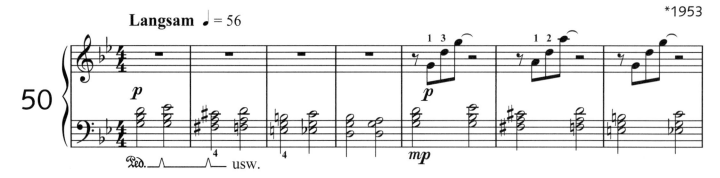

# Zwergentanz
## Dance of the Dwarfes

Rainer Mohrs
*1953

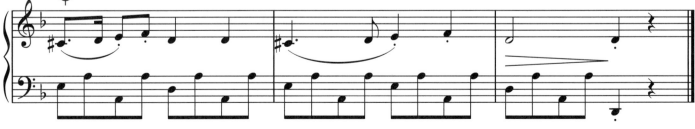

# Rock, Pop, Tango and more...
## Ferien / Holidays

Mike Schoenmehl
*1957

aus / from: M.Schoenmehl, Fun with Jazz Piano, Band 1 / Vol.1, Schott ED 8321

Die rechte Hand bewegt sich im Fünfton-Raum:

The right hand moves within this five-note position:

Die „vorgezogene 3" wird bei durchgehender Achtel -
zählweise erfahren. Die unterstrichenen Zählzeiten
können zunächst auch geklatscht werden. Immer laut
und gleichmäßig dabei zählen; das gilt auch für Takt 5
und 7.

The anticipated third beat can be mastered by counting
in quavers throughout. The counts underlined may first
be clapped. At the same time always count aloud and
evenly. This applies also to bars 5 and 7.

Die linke Hand spielt eine chromatische Linie von $c^1$
nach fis, ab- und aufwärts. Zuerst langsam üben. Es ist
auch möglich in der linken Hand Viertel statt Halbe zu
spielen. Das stabilisiert auch die Rhythmik in Takt 5
und 7.

The left hand plays a chromatic line from C to F sharp,
descending and ascending. First practise slowly. It is
also possible to play crotchets in the left hand instead
of quavers. This is especially beneficial for the rhythms
in bars 5 and 7.

# 12 Regenwetter-Blues / Rainy Weather Blues

Gunter Kretschmer
1935–2012

**Lässig / Nonchalantly** ♩. = 52

**53**

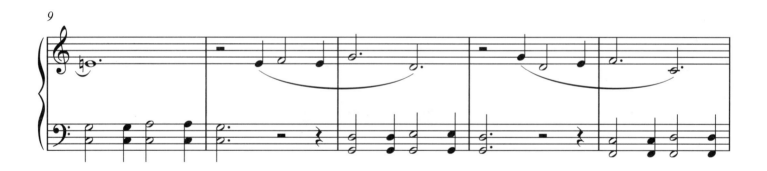

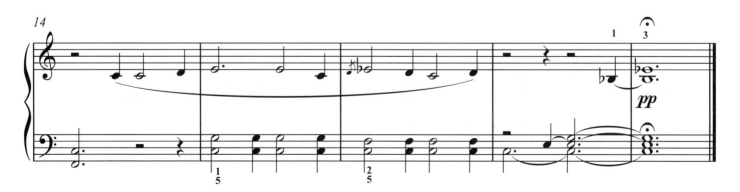

aus / from: G. Kretschmer, Auf dem Spielplatz / In the Playground, Schott ED 20648

# Ragtime

Georges Frank Humbert
1892–1958

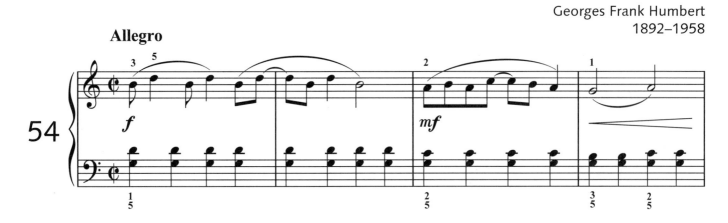

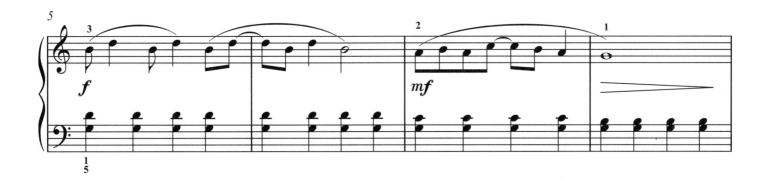

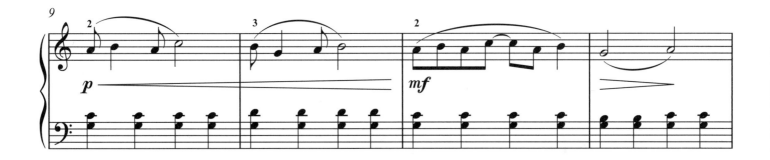

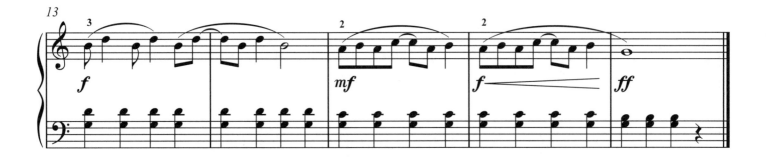

Originaltitel: Der tanzende Neger / The Dancing Negro

# Tango

Fritz Emonts
1920–2003

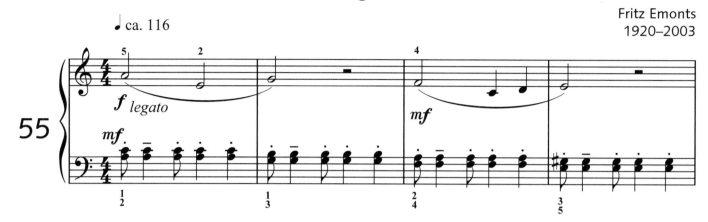

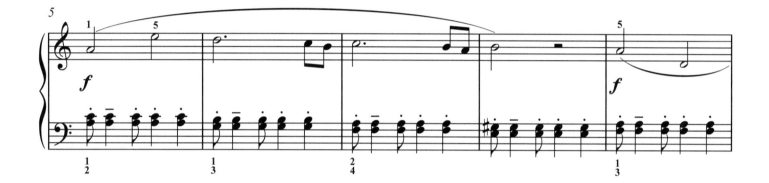

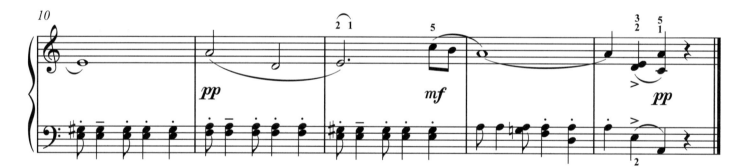

# Regentag / Rainy Day

Jürgen Moser
*1949

aus / from: J. Moser, Rock Piano, Band 1, Schott ED 7029

# Wenn ein Traum vergeht / When a Dream drifts away

George Nevada
*1939

aus / from: G. Nevada, Romantische Miniaturen / Romantic Miniatures, Schott ED 7696

Schott Music, Mainz 54 041